The romances and other poems

The romances and other poems
micah cavaleri

DEADMAN
PUBLISHING

Dollar Bay, Michigan
2012

ISBN 978-0-9827014-1-6

Dead Man Publishing, LLC
PO Box 349
Dollar Bay, MI 49922

special thanks to all who risked publishing my
work: *Bluestem, Bolts of Silk, elimae,
experimental-experiential-literature, New
Mystics and Short, Fast and Deadly*

for services rendered

lines from abya

if I a greenhouse in my heart had built

he told me if I a greenhouse
in my heart had built he told me
if I a greenhouse in my heart had built
he told me if I am a greenhouse in my heart.
had built a sunroom more and more
more and more and more
a sunroom so more until
he told me if I am greenhouse in my heart, had built
him in a sunroom, more and more.

ah, he did. he told me if I am a greenhouse in my
            heart
he was built, more and more, him a sunroom, more
            and more

in the spring he left

in the spring he left
his hand, the cool water,
lying flat on
his belly. no.
cool water, a smooth pothole in the rock.
if the pale blue sky ever changed
if the ponderosa sap sustains
a body,
he will be amber.
....

in the spring he left
in the spring he left
in the spring he left
me without a tent and the rain
April, the tree, in the spring he left
me without a tent and the rain
April, the tree limb from the wind
the breeze from the blossom at
him, he left,
me in the tree limb's breeze,
in April he left me without a tent and the rain
in the spring he left me

that was last spring barely april

but

that was last spring barely April
him a jeans a shirt a rope for a clothes line
him a last then a last you know
that was last spring barely April then
him a last shirt a rope of last spring clothes line
that was last spring barely April
him a spring flower shirt a rain of last spring
him a jeans verse a last rope a clothes

winter still here not a crocus

"winter still here not a crocus
"root still ground is a tomato
"seed still in her with a breath
"less still sheets"

white shoes in a wide grass or
white shoes in a wide lawn

white shoes in a field a friend
a fire in a forest, then
song, then

Come winter, a flower or a vegetable garden
will give in to you.

the romances

a plated steel monstrance
(for Aby Kaupang)

the yellow (yellow).

is simply ~~vibrant~~,
a (green) field
the field of
the air or whatever.
physical quantity.
Amen, amen,
to the man on
the bloddy tre
whose blood
makes the air.

...
I didn't know that my heart could rest in you.
Holy... I fail, every time. But I will kneel at the
          marble rail
to adore your tabernacle, a monstrance
          (monstrosity) of (baked) bread
I worship, my true God, a plated steel monstrance

finally a holy wooden
(for Martin Corless-Smith)

finally in a holy wooden
cross, cut from a tree
for the carving of a grotesque
hung body
of my god, (a lover
twisted
lover,) O my ~~(beaten)~~
~~god, O (my romance)~~

where on earth is your body? made of bread,
I will worship you (still) (monster) in a steel
monstrance, in ~~(a sacred beehive)~~
                         in a (sacred) sanctuary/behind
                         a (sacred)(yellow) rail

greenest nest
(for Rebecca Lilly)

what greenest (green) nest
built on the branch of a lonely tree
in a (yellow) yellow field?
the warbler
whistles a griblet~~(s)~~ after the light

my grandma as a kid
(for Molly)

in the leaves (the yellow leaves), I will write a maze
(a romantic) mist similar to the (green) strange
book I got at the (strange) store
with my grandma as a kid... "a brew of
          resemblances"
like a fairytale of a girl who finds immortality
in a drum.

the naturalist
(for Anne Gorrick)

I have finally come around
to write this book
of yellow and red illustrations
of green palms
only centuries late

How have I forgotten what I discovered
on a ship as if I was on a ship I forgot

Fried (green) plantains taste like (yellow) honey
although I did not
sit down to write
a cook book. These
illustrations are
illuminations of
a voyage I never
expected to make
until I saw the boards
of the hull. Now
I am lost at sea.

a glowing (a romantic)

a glowing (a romantic) globe
over the flooded river
a rising (a risen) light remains (remained)
near (nether or neither) a shore
where the tables reach out over
the dark water. Here is where (I swear) my lips
(my lisp) embarrasses my heart (the lack of art)
in what I say here at these tables, over
these retracting waters/ the raging river/
the romantic globe of light. [a leaf passed like a boat
too fast ...

a glowing (a romantic)

globes (glowing) retract from the surface
globes (glowing) from the retracting surface
a whale's song (he sang [or wrote])
the romance of the play of light

there are too far away
to walk to far where a cliff, a tree
there to there as a move
of earth's, a curve of black soil. There is a green
mold on the edge of a crack
between concrete slabs of
the sidewalk, an old path to
there, there, brown, the brown
and place.

a leaf (a dying)

a leaf (a dying dead Christ) erects a tree
(a romantic) (tree) yellow speaking to green
here you are there I am (strum theremin)
to disencumber (discover) lightness in fall
or some season with [an/the] absence of water

in this holy fragment (a romantic)

these holy fragments (and)
in these holy fragments
in this holy fragment is written
layers of numbers under words
on numbers then words
of (a palimpsest of) ancient languages
to reveal the eschaton's true color
a bright blue
it follows on a dull green (a palimpsest
is not a tempest, this is a tempest)
sky, a dull green sky
(a romantic) revelation

a piece of holy wood

a piece of holy wood, an aromatic (a romantic) piece
        of
wood. a grotesque piece of wood
is a wet offering
of my lost heart, my lost heart

augustine's conversion

now, in my hour of need,
my Lord on a wood
cross (on a tree)
remain(s) hung

i hear children
singing to pick up the book
and cry. i am weak.
i am weak. a grown man weeps
tearing his hair over philosophy
entities he's never seen, truth-values,
the adolescent romance of heaven.

if three words

If three words escape my mouth
most Green you, the Yellow field,
        O!   A plump buns
Your tree lifted in pain

up to a raging river hiding
        shiny, deep hidden things
shiny surface
(a romantic) surface of water

(escapes me)

China

I set out to find a romantic voice
in China (a verse) beside a green (verse)
~~a~~ river, a (yellow) river man
gave me a yellow ~~(poem~~ stitched ~~in a)~~ robe.

Under the river, the silt buried everything
but the day, and the swimmers
            a group of boys   and
girls swam in the water, the river
as the day ended. The tree on the bank
bent in front of the sun. The boys dressed.

the idea of a leaf

the idea of a leaf
that is spoken from a lip
with the slight spittle on a point
that is spoken in nothing
is a blue sky from a wider view   that
(closer/closure) is barely visible cotton
          on the head
          of a dandelion   closer/closure
closely slipping from the lips
speaking
with the spittle catches the edge of a leaf, invisibly

the closeness of ~~the word~~ (the wound)
under the blue sky, ~~(is)~~ the spittle is
blown over dandelion cottons catching on a leaf

these songs of delicate girls

these songs of delicate girls
recapture a romantic verse
as dark as water rushes
through sedge overflowing
beaches, the muddy banks
of exposed tree roots that
hang in the air like tree limbs,
the bottom of the silt river
buries a small light in its
indefinite soft flesh, their singing
their lost white limbs

these songs of delicate girls

these songs   these songs
of girls these (delightful) songs
of delicate girls to recapture (a romantic)
verse...

(an aperture) (romance) averse

to twins and rivers, and naked
in May, and the snow's still on the bank,

spying from the wood, my eye
is a sin (a song) of longing (a green)

                    romance (a romance)
                    (a yellow ~~romantic~~) romance

2 inch utterances

a field of white shoes   is a
field, a friend. A field is a
physical structure. A friend is
addressed. a field of white
shoes in the grass.

a harmony of bees and pikas in
a grass of wild flowers and
columbines is a human study of
release of cloud, sky, will

a milk bottle of grace[,/of] vastly
different life experiences
converge to a point momentarily

the anthropologie of flowers is
a simple girl scratching her
nose

here in three lines I write my
perfect fall where a small sign
breathes my only calm

O holy, forget, forget. Forget. O
holy forget. Here are the palms
of my hands.

O simple ethic, loving
beetles,

O my god, if you will uncut my
gut and hide my scar and make
me out of empty parts.

A very true prayer.

Where are the black orchids?
How can there be assassins? I
want my gun [back].

a fairytale

(a fairytale of) The Girl Called Ananaletheia Legein

In essence she is pleasant dressed in wool. In wool
and in pheasant and in gold. Her essence, pleasant,
calls in secret, calls in secret, calls the wind. Her
father whispers out the door that she is more than
wool.

Walking near a peccary the smell. But gold beneath
the loam
and wool. The loam is red and black and gold. She
sets her wool
on the ground
and that is where her pheasant sits
un un un
it breathes
barely hear the sound

Unwrap the wind from the sound and wool and there
she is, she is found
not a secret not a bird but a loam and gold

Her father whispers hear the word and there she is
in wool

She walks through the grass and kicks up gnats. In
the field near the river. The toucans sit in leather
leaves. The toucans never sing. But the yellow
eyelash viper hardly ever seen whispers as it coils
that the ants can sing. But their mouths are full.
Leaf clippings for the queen.

The rust and olive ants stretch out for miles from the
beach.

She sits at the beach by the ten foot mound
in wool
of loam
and gold
the ocean
her father whispers to sing

She takes a hand of sand. She walks back home.
The pleasant girl in wool. And in pheasant. And in
gold. The biting ants sting natural. Is the girl.
Pleasant dressed in wool.

tui tui

lake pond over lake pond

"The house the whole"
French when

French

the fish

tui
tui

lake pond
over   the reflection
lake pond

in the desert
to grow old speaking of poetry –
what is that like/what is it like? What
is a life of poetry? What is the life of
poetry? What is every word I speak
to you you hear from me you say to
me I hear from you I to you you to I
and I you and a pond a fire? does it
feel fluttery like the expectation of
reading poetry for sixty more years?
Is the expectation rather the poetics?
and then. and then.

a objet-a, to learn a word is to learn a concept. it
does not matter how it's use'd. I am use'd and en(d)
use may. I love a little letter and dive in.

I dove into the Raga/Strega, my grandmama, and
Bel and the Dragon. And there I found
I dive down in the book
to hide in a stem
of the letter 'b'

                        O My, my dream – as if I am moving
                        through a baby's single muttered cry

                                  (each movement
is slow)

I return to the open poem,
and the metaphysics

from the ashes of plants
alkahest

and aaliyah, return
to the desert

with the universal solvent
solent, a being and a whole

there, there, in the desert
alone

a baby a poem a shoe
from a friend, the frame

reaches around them as
the us is not in frame

except for my hands. I pray.
In the desert, grass and open

empty is a body
o my I rest o.

desert. I am a lake pond
                over   the reflection
              lake pond

No French, speak French and as an old woman,
speak to me tree, apple tree, climbing tree, thick low
limbs I climb a tree speak just speak just speak just
speak just speak just voice limb

o my your voice is an expectation

www.ingramcontent.com/pod-product-compliance
Lightning Source LLC
Chambersburg PA
CBHW072039060426
42449CB00010BA/2358